Lessons from My Path

Tess Kirby

Lessons from My Path

Tess Kirby

2014
Pathwork Press
Madison, VA

Pathwork Press
P.O. Box 725
Madison, VA 22727
www.pathwork.org

Cover Art *Through the Trees (spring version)* 2014© Rachel Willock www.racheyjaneprintsagain.com
Author Photo: Kat Foley
Cover & text design and production: L. Zoë Willow

—In service to life—

Dedicated with love and gratitude to all my teachers.

Table of Contents

Preface ix
Riding No Handed 1
Potent Prayers 3
Something Better 5
Spiritual Growth Related to Emotional Growth 7
The Danger and Promise of Feelings 9
Arriving Home 11
Tuning In 15
What Do I Need to Learn from This? 17
I Don't Want to Grow Up 19
I Do and I Don't 23
Our Little One Within 25
The Grapevines of Our Lives 27
Three Sacred Aspects 31
Gossip 33
A Steady Flow of Grace 37
Happiness and a Chain of Pain 39
Receiving Our Good 43
Divine Essence in Our Imperfections 45
Don't Hit 47
Dangerous Rules 49
Challenge the Rules 53
I Want to Want To 57
Getting Rid of Guilt 59
Connection 61
Anxiety and Hopelessness 63
Impatience 65

Blame 67
The Road to Freedom 71
"Forgot Your Dry Cleaning Again?" 73
Duality 75
Broken Heart 79
Tending 81
Making a Change 83
I'd Rather Not Today 85
A Time for Each 87
The Big Three 89
I Want What I Want When I Want It 93
Meeting Evil 97
Worry 99
It's Mostly about Me 101
A Matter of Perspective 105
Holding It All 107
You Can't Go Home Again . . . Although You Try and Try and Try 109
Forgot to Be Grateful 111
Nice Surprise!! 113
The Answer Will Come 115
Setting Intention 117
Who Am I? 119
About the Author 121

Preface

So many of us yearn for something better, something more. We're not sure what's missing; we just know that it is something. We find ourselves stuck in the same troubling situations over and over but can't figure out why. Happiness seems fleeting and life often feels empty and frustrating.

Once upon a time this was a pretty accurate description of my life.

I was walking a rocky road feeling anxious and lonely. I'd been raised as a go-to-church-7-days-a-week Catholic which left me feeling angry about religion and spirituality. As a young woman I was a single Mom responsible for my sons from the time they were very young. I felt helpless and alone and wished desperately to be rescued.

In the meantime, I lived my life as best I could. Eventually, from the outside, it looked pretty good. I had a successful career I loved as a management consultant and speaker, enjoyable travel, the boys were doing fine. I'd published a couple of books, had nice friends and dated interesting men. What more could I want? Well, . . . it turns out I wanted a whole lot more.

What I wanted was peace in my heart, a stomach and head that didn't hurt all the time and to have that horrible ache of loneliness gone. All things I believed it would be impossible to have.

Lessons from My Path is a collection of some of the practices which enabled me to move from that painful existence into the life I thought unattainable. A life filled much of the time with love, peace, health, happiness and true connection.

By the simple act of asking humbly for help, my rich life was on its way. Some help appeared in the form of a work colleague who introduced me to Unity Church where I learned to drop my anger at the spiritual world. It came in the form of my transcendental meditation teacher who showed up in a navy blue suit and pearls. It arrived in the form of a down-to-earth counselor who helped me begin to navigate my emotional world. It came in the form of countless teachers who introduced me to a world of generous spirit. It turned up as I stumbled across Pathwork teachings that served as the key for me to clear out a lot of tangled thinking that was tripping me up and holding me back from a truly fulfilling life.

I am enormously grateful for all the assistance, seen and unseen, that arrived to help me straighten out big chunks of my life and introduce my heart to love and kindness.

I was inspired to write *Lessons* out of a desire to share that abundance. I particularly want to thank Brian

O'Donnell, Margit Colagrande and Tara Welles for their encouragement and support. The format is the result of my desire to offer practical spiritual practices in a concise, easy-to-access style. Some days a simple reminder of a simple practice does the trick. At other times a bit more in-depth understanding is called for. Often we'd like a practical next step to take. A lot of times we need just a whisper of hope. My desire is that *Lessons from My Path* will meet all those needs for you as you create a life filled with genuine happiness, true love and deep connection with your soul.

For those of you who would like to have a more in-depth understanding of the Pathwork teachings presented I have referenced the names and numbers of lectures on some of the topics in this book which are available at www.pathwork.org

With blessings and love as you walk your path,

Tess Kirby
Ann Arbor, Michigan
October 2013

1

Riding No Handed

Driving home the other night I spotted a man riding his bike *no handed*. His arms were stretched wide and he had a huge smile on his face. I smiled too when it occurred to me that this is what my life is like a lot of the time these days. My arms open to life. I'm balanced, steady, gliding along with a smile, happy to be on earth. What a miracle.

For many years, I was depressed, frightened, angry and lonely. Stomach pains and headaches tortured me. I'd reached the point of toying with thoughts of suicide. I'm so glad I was willing to receive the help that had been waiting in the wings for my call.

My young sons pulled me back from the brink. Thank goodness I realized through my haze of pain that I loved them too much to desert them. Then, one evening, Mother Nature gave me a gift of hope through a stunning sky filled with incredible colors and cloud formations. It dawned on me, "If there's something powerful enough to create that magnificence, there's something powerful enough to get me out of my pain." Then, I whispered, "Help. Please."

Help was delivered in the practical and blessed form of a down to earth counselor. I drew on my courage to help me face my total self. With her assistance I started turning my life around by getting acquainted with me.

It turns out I wasn't so frightened of life because of other people or of what I thought I might encounter. I was frightened of me. I was frightened by my thoughts and frightened by my feelings. Up to that point my solution was to run away by ignoring, denying or stifling my emotions when they popped up.

Without being willing to look at what I was thinking and feeling, I had led my life in a disconnected way. Hidden thoughts and emotions were creating effects in my life that made me miserable but I wasn't connecting the dots. Once I started to identify my mistaken beliefs, I gained control. I could make choices to make my life better if I wanted to. And I did. The critical choice I made was to work to untangle my thinking and belief patterns. The result is that my life has been rich with happiness, safety and pleasure for quite a while now.

A fabulous bonus is that I found the way to my soul. All the debris I'd created from avoiding my thinking and beliefs prevented me from connecting with my inner wisdom as well as accessing my deep reservoir of love. By becoming acquainted with myself, I paved the way to create the life I had yearned for but had thought impossible to have.

2

Potent Prayers

The most potent prayers I know are *Please, Help,* and *Thank You.*

Please puts energy into motion. When you say, *Please,* you've set an intention, decided upon a request, figured out something you'd like to invite into your life that is important to you. The clarity and focus help it come to life.

Help is a wonderful way of letting the Universe know you realize that you can't produce the best results on your own. This humility goes a long way toward keeping you grounded and attracting constructive, inspired assistance. Guardians and guides who want nothing more than to have the honor of helping us surround us. This help can be solicited for not only our big ticket items but our small help-me-deal-with-the-bumps-in-the-road-today requests.

Thank you is a simple expression of gratitude—gratitude for the help—gratitude for the results. Not only does expressing our appreciation attract even more abundance, it is a genuine way of connecting with peace and happiness as well as a great reminder that we are already rich in so many ways.

3

Something Better

I've created a small altar in a corner of my kitchen next to my coffee pot. It's there to remind me of a truth I sometimes forget. That truth is that if we allow it, the Universe will often deliver something to us much better than we ever could think of ourselves. This altar reminds me of the many times this has happened in my life.

I wanted a job that would support my family and that I wouldn't consider drudgery. I ended up with a career I loved in a field that I didn't even know existed until the Universe said, "Here. Have some fun. Try this." I yearned to raise my family in a home I could afford in an area we would enjoy. We found the perfect house in the perfect neighborhood for a price that fit my budget. I always wanted to write a book. A publisher accepted my proposal within a week of sending it out. Money and travel dropped in my lap. Fun bargains showed up. Fortunately the list goes on and on.

I have the altar there because sometimes I forget. I particularly forget in the middle of the night when I'm most vulnerable. That's why the strategic placement of my altar next to the coffee pot. In seeking out the comfort of my morning coffee, I am reminded of the greater comfort. I pray my prayer of, "Please provide the best I can think of or something better."

The Universe has delivered over and over. Why should my future be any different than my past?

4

Spiritual Growth Related to Emotional Growth

A critical part of our spiritual development is helping our souls grow into wholeness by healing the bumps, gashes and wounds they've collected over the ages. We pull that off by dipping into our emotional life and squarely facing what creates the dense and tangled undergrowth on the path to our real selves. Honestly confronting our feelings, our motivations, our desires, and our faults not only soothes our souls but also paves the way for achieving emotional maturity.

The amazing beauty of this process is that the act of chopping our way inch by inch through the undergrowth is exactly how we grow up. Our emotional strength grows with each act of courageously facing ourselves.

By restoring our souls to their original perfection, we find out what incredible beings we are. The great news is that we don't have to wait for the job to be complete before we can enjoy the benefits. As we tend the wounds, we're able to tap into the infinite wisdom, peace, security and happiness that our souls possess. [1]

---

1 PWL # 141, "Return to the Original Level of Perfection"

5

The Danger and Promise of Feelings

Our feelings endanger us, not by their mere existence, but by our choosing to keep them hidden from ourselves. When we're not aware of what we feel and believe, we live from a disconnected place unknowingly detonating land mines again and again.

By not being in touch with our inner, unconscious world, we and everyone else in our lives, live with the danger of our hidden feelings leaking out in ways that are often cruel and destructive.

Another by-product of hiding from our feelings is that the emotions we repress can contribute powerfully to our life experience. The result is that we undergo crisis and disappointment over and over. Mistakenly, we blame the situation for the strong emotions we're experiencing, while it actually works the other way around. The feelings we've tamped down create the turmoil. For example, as a young woman I wasn't able to sustain a healthy relationship with a man. I kept thinking that lack of a good relationship was the reason I felt so miserable. It actually was just the opposite. I couldn't have a good relationship because I felt so miserable as a result of distorted thinking that I wasn't aware of.

When we ignore our feelings, anger grows. We blame other people and circumstances for not allowing us to have the kind of life that we think will be the answer to our problems. If only *they* or *it* would get out of our way, we could be happy forever.

Not attending to our feelings backfires because we're asking for the impossible. We hope we can be connected with others and interact with the world in a satisfying way while we hide behind a thick wall of denial and phoniness.

To remove the danger and stop the pain, we need to meet our emotions head on. Once we're in touch with the true nature of our feelings, we realize we have nothing to fear by facing them. Looking at them removes their destructive power. The more we're connected to our feelings, the more we learn to deal with them constructively. We figure out how to interact beneficially with the right people at the right time in the right place. We come to understand how crises and other nasty events came about and how it's in our power to create a much better future. Being clued in to our feelings gives us the power to experience genuine happiness.[2]

2 Pathwork Lectures #183 and #190

6

Arriving Home

When we connect with ourselves, contentment and confidence wash through us. We recognize with great pleasure, "Ah, finally home." To get to that place, it's important to listen to all the voices that live in us. Many of the messages from our brain, history, fears and hopes create static that gets in the way of hearing what our soul is offering. Before we can hear that soul voice, which is certainly the one we want to access, we need to eliminate the static or at least control it. The best way I've found to do that is to give it a voice.

Listening to all the messages is important because until we know what we're whispering to ourselves, they unconsciously control our lives. When we finally connect with some of the things going through our heads, we often feel our jaws drop and hear our brains protest, "Of course I'm not thinking such ridiculous things." Instead of chastising ourselves for what we're thinking and feeling, it's in our best interests to accept it. It's there for a reason. The more we listen to what we say to ourselves the more we'll have compassion for the child within us who mistakenly believes these things. Then we're able to connect the dots between what we think and what is happening in our lives.

For example, as I started uncovering my hidden thinking, I was surprised to learn that I believed relationships were dangerous. The result was that on the surface I invited friendship. Then, unbeknownst to them or me, I began pushing people away the moment the relationship threatened to become too close. It was only a matter of time until I could find a deal breaker that gave me a *good* reason to end it. In my attempt to be safe, I chased people away even though I consciously thought I wanted nothing more than to connect. Once I knew this, I had a map to explore why I felt this way and what I could do to bring about more positive results. This is how I gained the ability to create a better life. I learned to pay attention to me which led the way for me to be in touch with the deeper wisdom of my soul.

Being in touch with what our soul is saying takes effort but it's not as difficult as our darker self would like us to believe. This shadowy self is the part of us that really doesn't want us to give our best to life. This unenlightened aspect has a great investment in keeping our attention focused on the static. The power of this shady self is threatened by our intention to connect with our souls. The energy contained in our lower/shadow self is in reality divine energy that has gotten distorted. As we listen to our soul's guidance the distortions clear up as the energy is transformed back into its divine state. Once that's done, the lower self has no power. No wonder our lower natures fight hard to keep us from being in touch with our divine reality.

To begin to make that soul connection, a first step is to let ourselves and the Universe know that this is what we want to do. The first time I did that was when, in despair, I wrote the word "Help," on the first page of a large red journal. I didn't open that journal for another three years but the message was sent and received and help was on the way.

7

Tuning In

Our life is a living picture of what is going on for us internally. It's critical to connect with our inner world because we constantly create from there. Our thoughts and feelings determine whether we create in a constructive, loving way or in a negative, destructive manner.

Here are a few suggestions to help you get in touch with what's you're thinking and feeling.

One simple approach is to make a date with yourself at the end of the day to go over the events of the day. See how you feel about what happened. After you've done this for a while, go back over your notes and look for what trends pop out. This gives you a great jumping off point to start working more deeply on issues if you choose.

Another way is to begin the day as Julia Cameron, author of *The Artist's Way*, suggests. She encourages people to write three pages of free-form thoughts first thing every morning. Since we are closest to our subconscious and unconscious thoughts when we first awaken, we can tap into a mother lode of information about ourselves. Capturing what emerges in writing keeps it from slipping away.

Meditation is of course another marvelous way to turn within to meet your heart and soul.

A powerful way to listen to yourself is to talk to another person without editing what you're saying. This person can be a trusted friend who has the same goals as you do in terms of spiritual growth, a counselor, a spiritual teacher. Alone, you may be locked in a vacuum that blocks self-understanding. If you can open to another, the vacuum seal is broken and understanding has a chance to flow.

If there isn't someone in your midst so far that fills this bill or you're not ready to open up to someone else yet, don't be concerned. Just let the Universe know you're looking for a spiritual friend to partner with for your growth and that person will appear at the perfect time in your development.

8

What Do I Need to Learn from This?

We attract the situations we experience because we have something to learn from them. Life on earth is one big campus and every event is a custom-made class. It truly is a perfect system. The hitch is that we don't necessarily dive into our inner life with an attitude of "Oh boy! There's something to learn here. Let's not waste any time getting to it." It's more often a case of running the other way, figuring a time bomb is loaded to go off if we start messing around in there.

Well, the time bomb is in there but the only way it gets set off is if we neglect to disarm it by taking an honest look at ourselves. We take the power out of the bomb by examining our motivations, desires and disgruntlements along with taking responsibility for our part in creating whatever has happened.

When I'm caught up in a challenging or painful situation, I try to remember to ask myself "What do I need to learn from this?" Until I remember to ask that question I stay tangled up tripping over myself and taking others down with me. This is a great habit to develop.

9

I Don't Want to Grow Up

When we're emotionally mature we experience security, self-confidence and self-respect. We're comfortable in the world and things flow easily. We interact from a genuine connection with others and ourselves. There's a wonderful feeling of strength and happiness. With all these benefits, why do most of us fight so hard against growing up? The main reason is that being emotionally mature requires us to be on speaking terms with our feelings. That punches our panic button. How come?

One reason is that when we're young we learn to associate having feelings with danger and pain. We do this because our parents, as well as others in authority, often didn't do a very good job of coping with our strong emotions and needs because of their own lack of emotional maturity. Between their panicky reactions and often some kind of punishment doled out in an attempt to control us, we erroneously concluded that emotional life is treacherous territory. As a way to avoid pain and danger, we made the decision to disconnect from our feelings any way we could.

We hold another unconscious belief from childhood which is that having a feeling and acting it out go hand in hand. Every now and then we accidentally get a glimpse of some of these strongly repressed feelings that live in us. It scares us when we think of the mayhem we would cause and the trouble that would come our way if we acted on these feelings. So, we refuse to take a look at them. As we mature emotionally, we learn that being aware of a feeling and acting on it are two separate things. In fact, when we're aware of what we're feeling, we have control over how to deal with it. It's when we're not aware of the full range of our feelings that we act out destructively.

We also resist looking at our emotions because this threatens our phony self-image. When we face ourselves we see all sorts of faults and imperfections living alongside our good qualities. Deep inside we believe that dropping the pretense of perfection actually means our total annihilation so we fight tooth and nail not to go there.

Another reason we balk at growing up emotionally is that we don't want to deal with the learning curve that's involved. Yes indeed, emotional growth has a learning curve just like physical prowess or mental achievement. We stumble and make mistakes and grow stronger and more adept as a result of dealing with those mistakes. The part of us that wishes we were perfect right now fights this process, another part believes it's dangerous to make mistakes and yet another part is just plain lazy and doesn't want to do the work.

No wonder we're reluctant to face our feelings.[3]

3 Pathwork Lecture 89 Emotional Growth and Its Function

10

I Do and I Don't

As seekers on a spiritual path, we learn that if we envision what we want, the law of attraction will deliver it to our doorstep. This is true but it's only half the equation when we're dealing with how we create.

Sometimes the Universe delivers just what we pictured or better. At times though, we get mighty disappointed. Is this because we don't deserve to have our dreams come true? Did we not ask correctly? Did we ask for too much? Do we need to negotiate a bit? Are we being punished? The answer is none of the above. The reason is that, on an unconscious level, we might be saying *no* to what we ardently yearn for.

We'll ask for things that on the surface seem terrific and reasonable. Who could argue with requesting a loving partner, prosperity, peace of mind or good relationships? As we untangle the knots of our unconscious thinking, we can begin to understand why our hearts' desires remain elusive.

Entwined in there with a yearning for a loving partner may be the fear that we won't be able to take care of ourselves in a relationship. Twisted in with a desire for prosperity could be a fear that we're not really worthy of having abundance. Tucked in there with a desire for peace of mind might be the belief that a lack of chaos with its drama could be boring. idden within wanting to be in relationship with others could be a fear that they might find us lacking and ultimately reject us. So, in a misguided attempt to protect ourselves, we unconsciously say the deadly *no* to having our dreams fulfilled.

Sometimes it's a struggle to even consider the possibility that we're pushing away the very thing we want so dearly. When this happens, it helps to pray for the willingness to look at the complete picture . . . all the parts that are saying, *yes* and all the parts that are saying *no*. Drawing on our courage to explore whether we might have an unconscious *no* to fulfillment lessens its grip and begins to clear the way to finally attaining what we really want.

11
Our Little One Within

When we were young, we coped with life as best we could using a child's limited logic. The conclusions and solutions drawn from that immature reasoning got stored in our unconscious. As long as it remains unconscious we continue to unknowingly operate from this child's logic and pain.

Our Little One

is self centered.
wants what it wants when it wants it.
demands exclusive, unconditional love.
never wants to feel any pain or discomfort.
want to be happy 110% of the time.
is vulnerable.
is wounded.

If our Little One doesn't experience life on its terms it

has temper tantrums.
digs in its heels.
tries every trick in the book to get its way.

Our Little One grows into maturity through our

acknowledgement
respect
protection
nurturing
understanding

The best part of us lives in the yearnings of our Little One:

our longing to love and be loved
our generosity
our excitement
our joy
our desire to squander ourselves into life

The Little One needs to be coaxed to come out. Blame, impatience or anger doesn't do the trick. The Little One blossoms into maturity and health through our compassionate desire to understand and nurture that vulnerable, incredible part of us. Exploring the world of our Little One provides a mother lode of information about why our life is turning out the way it is.

12

The Grapevines of Our Lives

Someone decided long before I bought my home that grapevines in the backyard tucked up against the garage would be a good idea. Not being much of a gardener and someone who thought the grape leaves were pretty, I didn't do much to tend them. Result? Grapevines aggressively took root in my backyard so that grape leaves have replaced grass in an awful lot of my back lawn. Well, a couple of weeks ago I decided that something needed to be done . . . therefore, armed with a pair of sharp shears, gloves and a pitcher of lemonade I proceeded to tackle this miniature jungle. It turned out to be a wonderful illustration of a spiritual journey.

End Goal

Put the grapevines back where they belong so that things would be the way they're supposed to be . . . beautiful, functional, safe, and pleasurable.

Present Condition

Grape vines and leaves running amok, taking over territory they never were intended to control, spreading through invasive growth, cutting off the light to the plants and grass. Fun is squashed because we can't play there anymore. Golf balls, baseballs, badminton birdies, croquet balls get swallowed up if they hit the leaves. Running for tag is out because the grapevines trip us up and the growth up the side of my garage is threatening to topple that whole structure.

What I Found as I Proceeded to Chop Away

The grapevines are pretty on the outside. As I lifted up a bunch of leaves and vines though, the underside was tangled and dark with lots more deadness than aliveness. I also found that as I cut and cut the pile of debris grew tall but it didn't seem like I was getting very far very fast. Then, at some point in the process . . . I'd grab hold of a vine and as I pulled, up would come a root. Some of these roots were ten feet long . . . some about an inch in diameter. With the unearthing of this root, a whole patch of dirt was exposed to the light. Finally, the soil could breathe, have sunshine, moisture, warmth and I could plant something wonderful.

Why This Is Like a Spiritual Journey

What we don't expose to the light spreads aggressively. Yes, it can look pretty on the surface. But, when a distorted belief or idea gets implanted it produces destructive growth in that dark place. The only way to stop it in its malicious tracks is to expose it to the light. Once exposed, things can be the way they were originally intended: safe, pleasurable, functional, beautifully alive . . . thriving.

A powerful step in spiritual growth is to chop away at mistaken thoughts and beliefs that take over your life and produce darkness and deadness.

Chopping may take a while before you get to the root. Sometimes it can feel like you're not making much progress. Then, the root is found. The feeling of peace that comes when it is pulled out so it can't do any more damage is fantastic. Finally there is fertile soil to cultivate a lovely, pleasurable, safe, healthy life.

13

Three Sacred Aspects

As we grapple with life's challenges, it's helpful to be aware of three aspects of ourselves.

One dimension wants us to give our best to life. This is the part that prompts us to live in love, kindness, generosity and honesty. It's the aspect that promotes growth, healing and constructive creation.

Another part is a darker/shady side that tempts us to cheat life and hurt others. It's that part of us that works against our yearning to connect, grow and heal.

The third in this trio doesn't want to suffer any consequences for behaving badly. The goal of this side is to make us look good to ourselves and everyone else. It's the part of us that takes on the job of providing *good* reasons when we behave poorly or act downright cruelly. This is the aspect that uses good reasons to blame as well.

For example, let's say someone hurts me somehow . . ..

In my reaction, the darker side of me wants to hurt them back. The part that rationalizes will come up with several excuses that would make it seem reasonable to lash out at them in response. The part of me that wants to give my best will prompt me to look at this situation honestly and with good intentions. That would entail taking a look at my part in the situation. I also could consider what might have been going on for them or think about what I'd like for an outcome that could be mutually beneficial.

Paying attention to all three aspects gives us the power to make a conscious choice of how we want to be in life . . . genuinely giving our best or behaving badly and making excuses for it. [4]

4 Pathwork Lecture 14 The Higher Self, the Lower Self, and the Mask

14

Gossip

I dismayed and shocked myself by gossiping this morning . . ..

I'm not a gossip. I checked with my friends to make sure I wasn't deluding myself. They all said, "No—I don't experience that with you."

So what the heck happened? Gossiping is something I'm extremely uncomfortable with. I felt terrible that I had had shared information about another that was none of my business to be sharing. While I was doing it . . . actually, even before I shared, I stopped myself and asked, "Hmmm, ... Is it okay for me to tell this?" I quickly came up with an accommodating, *Yes*, and proceeded to betray my friend.

Gossip isn't just sharing information, it has a nasty delicious twist to it. There's a dark pleasure in passing on another's bad fortune. I could feel that smiling, mean energy. The juicy pleasure of dipping my toes into the gossip pond lasted about as long as it took me to pass on the news. After I ended that conversation, a number of emotions I don't like to experience rushed in: anxiety, guilt, gnawing emptiness.

After I managed to put my anger and distress with myself aside and sincerely ask the question, "What happened?" I found some enlightening and humbling things.

For several reasons this phone call from this particular friend had activated my Little One who so desperately craves love and attention and a feeling of being special but doesn't believe it's ever going to come her way. My darker side saw an opportunity and latched on. Result?

Below my conscious level I was so grateful this person had made the effort to contact me that I thought I had to give her something *really good* in return for doing me the favor of taking notice of me. I also wanted to have that I'm-so-important-I'm-in-the-know feeling. In addition, I found I also wanted that feeling of exclusivity and, in this instance, I got a two-for-one deal. I could feel special about my connection with the friend I betrayed because she had shared this confidence with me and I could demonstrate that *specialness* to my friend on the phone. Supposedly, this created a special pact between us too.

What I find most astounding and informative about this experience is how easily I fell into doing this evil act that is not on my regular list of temptations. I found I got thrown off base because the phone call came early in the morning before I had gotten grounded through my spiritual practice. My darker side moved right in to take advantage. It was a good lesson to see how easily I can stumble when I'm not connected to myself.

15

A Steady Flow of Grace

Occasionally, we get a glimpse of how powerful our soul's help can be. Often though, the arrival of assistance can feel like a hit or miss proposition. Sometimes we receive help when we can only whisper the word. Other times it seems we can bang on the door forever and still feel left out in the cold.

On my path I've learned that it turns out it's not a hit or miss proposition after all. We just need to bring three things to the table in order to consistently experience grace and gifts beyond measure.

First, we need to dig up some willpower to say, "Yes, I'm willing to meet some parts of me that have been hidden." The knots in our souls are tight. The lazy part of us says, "Untangling these knots seems like a lot of work. Let's not go there." So, it does require our commitment of saying, "Yes, I choose to venture into this territory of meeting my real self."

Second, it helps a lot if you make an investment of time every day. Spiritual work is similar to tending our bodies. Without attention, layers of dirt build up and disease takes hold. With regular hygiene and nourishment, our beauty and health grow. It's the same with our souls. Their growth needs to be nurtured and honored. At the beginning of my journey, I greatly resisted devoting any committed time to my spiritual growth. I had a lot of "good reasons" why I couldn't. Among them . . . building a career, being back in school, single motherhood, homeownership, being a friend. I was operating under the mistaken assumption that my spiritual life was separate from my *real* life.

Finally, thank goodness, I committed to work with my soul's growth for twenty minutes a day. I know someone else who began with five minutes a day. It's not how much time you spend that gets the process started; it's the commitment.

Third is the willingness to bring some common sense and compassion to our soul work. In the beginning we can get tangled up in judgments and negative thinking about how we've lived our lives and go down that distracting path. We need to treat ourselves with kindness and our darker side with objectivity.

As I got more in touch with my inner self, it became obvious that my outer problems and challenges were merely a reflection of my inner ones. Once I resolved the inner conflicts, my outer ones disappeared. Hand in hand came self-confidence, security and an ability to enjoy life.

16

Happiness and a Chain of Pain

Strange as it seems, we attempt to gain happiness, security and self-confidence in a way that actually creates anxiety, depression and fear instead. How did things get so turned around?

When we were young, we learned that being thought of as *good* brought a lot more pleasure and acceptance our way than when we were considered *not good*. We also knew that we weren't able to be perfect which, with our childish reasoning, was our definition for good. In an attempt to find a solution to this dilemma of believing we needed to be perfect but knowing we weren't, we unconsciously created a phony self that pretended to be all the things that we thought would identify us as good. We were hopeful that if we could convince the world . . . maybe even ourselves . . .we were this false version of perfection, we'd have our ticket to happiness, self-confidence and security. This erroneous belief remains in our unconscious until we unearth it and our phony self lives on unless we unmask it.

Accompanying this idealized, false version of ourselves

is a tyrant who has the job of making sure we live up to our outlandish and impossible standards. When we fall short, as we must, the tyrant intensifies efforts to force us to be *perfect*. This of course meets with failure and we feel even more miserable and insecure. So, as we try harder and harder to perfect this phony version of ourselves, we get even more depressed and anxious. As we hide our real selves behind this phony facade, we feel guilty for living a lie. In addition, shame and fear of exposure are building which leads to even more anxiety, depression and fear. We get pretty angry too. We're trying so hard to be "good." Why isn't it working? It isn't working because none of it is based in reality.

One step toward breaking this chain of pain is to risk meeting your phony self. A way to begin is to identify some of the outlandish standards and demands you've set for yourself. As you look at them objectively you'll see their total impossibility. In my case, I discovered that I'd invested a lot of effort to be thought of as upbeat, interesting and entertaining. I did this in hopes of being accepted and admired, which I thought would lead to happiness and self-confidence.

When I investigated what I meant by "upbeat, interesting and entertaining" I found that I thought each time I was with people I needed to:

> Offer informed, intelligent opinions about any topic that might come up.
>
> Amuse others with funny anecdotes.

Relate fascinating tales about glamorous experiences I've had.

Astound with my wit.

Impress by being culturally well-rounded as well as athletically accomplished.

I find it remarkable that just by the act of identifying what impossible-to-meet criteria I'd imposed upon myself, I freed the tyrant to drop the whip and stop trying to beat me into being *perfect*.

Another helpful thing is to consider whether your outlandish standards could be the reason you feel anxious and/or depressed at times. When you feel miserable, instead of looking to find an outside source to blame or allowing the bully to try to whip you into shape, look to see if it's possible that you may be trying to live up to some impossible-to-meet self-imposed demands.

Another way out of this pain is to be willing to become acquainted with your total self where imperfections live alongside good qualities. By doing this, we give ourselves the opportunity to see where we are genuinely *good* and work constructively with the parts that we feel are genuinely *not good*. Once I decided to give up my act, not only did I discover some appealing things about myself, but I paved the way to true friendship.

When we have the courage to meet ourselves in

our wonderfulness with our humanity and are brave enough to unmask our phony self, we experience the fresh air of freedom and safety. We can finally rest because we're in touch with our center which is the only secure place to be. We can finally grow, because growth can only occur from that part of our being. By releasing our phony selves, we meet what life offers in a different way. We can finally experience true self-confidence, strength and happiness.[5]

5 Pathwork Lecture 83 The Idealized Self-Image

17

Receiving Our Good

At times, it's difficult to downright impossible to receive our good because we're holding out clenched fists to catch it. These are the times when we invite some wonderful thing into our lives because we're afraid of dealing with its opposite.

We ask for a partner because we're afraid of being on our own.

We ask for money because we're frightened of poverty.

We ask for intelligence because we're afraid of appearing stupid.

We ask for peace because we're afraid of violence.

We ask for success because we're terrified of feeling like a failure.

We ask for self-confidence because we're afraid of dealing with our insecurities and their causes.

The law of the Universe says we can have anything we want as long as we're willing to accept its opposite. Unless we face what we fear, we keep the door to our abundance bolted shut. Once we can say *yes*, to all of it, our fists will unclench and we have the possibility of obtaining our heart's desires.

One way to help open our hands to receive is to ask for help and compassion in understanding our fears. We might ask some questions like:

> "What would happen if the opposite of what I want happened instead?"
>
> "Would that be as awful as I'm projecting?"
>
> "Could there be some alternatives I've not considered?"[6]

6 Pathwork Lecture 155 Fear of Self—Giving and Receiving

18

Divine Essence in Our Imperfections

Our imperfections and good qualities originate from the same divine energy. This is an easy thing to forget as we stumble along the path to meet our soul. Imperfections are the result of positive energy getting twisted and kinked in a misguided effort to protect ourselves. The work of spiritual transformation is to straighten out those kinks and have the energy flow in its beautiful, pure, original constructive form. It's a great practice and gift for ourselves to occasionally pay a bit of attention to this truth.

A good beginning step is to make a list of some of our imperfections and good qualities.

While creating this list it can be helpful to ask someone who knows us well what they think of us. We need to let them know we're working on improving ourselves and would appreciate their honesty. It's important to make an effort to listen with an open mind and keep a lid on our defensiveness.

Once we have a few things on our list we're often surprised when we ask ourselves:

"What messages do these imperfections and good qualities bring to me?"

"What divine aspect is behind each distortion?"

I've found it helpful to write down what I learn—it comes in handy when I need a reminder.

Some I found are:

My anger is linked to striving for justice

I manipulate out of the mistaken belief that this is my only way to have abundance

My stubbornness stems from my willingness to stand firm

My false pride is linked with my desire to be truly proud of myself

My grasping can be linked to a desire to claim my good.[7]

7 Pathwork Lecture 148 Positivity and Negativity: One Energy Current

19

Don't Hit

One of the first things we tell little ones as we pull them away from each other during a tussle is, "Don't hit." I'm thinking that's probably pretty good advice for my Little One right now too.

I was hurt by someone this week. I wanted to hit them in response. So I am. Not physically, but I find I'm telling my tale of woe to any of my friends who will listen. Of course, my version is being told in such a way so that they want to hit her too. I don't feel good about myself after I do it, but I continue to talk about this anyway. I'm having a lot of trouble resisting this temptation to lash out.

Hitting others through words or physical acts is aggressive and violent. This feeds right into the evil of separating from others and myself. It provides a momentary, delicious charge. That charge is quickly followed by feeling deflated, sad and isolated. I don't like myself very well when I behave badly like this and I want to hit me too.

As I'm working to sort this out, I'm realizing there's a lot that I don't understand about this situation. I do know one thing though . . . as I muddle my way through this dilemma, "Don't hit," would probably be a good place to start.

I'd love to be choosing to do the right thing because I feel loving and compassionate. Well, right now, I don't. I still feel hurt and angry and vengeful.

I'm committed to sorting this through but it looks like that could take a while.

So right now, I remind myself that the smart plan of action to begin to climb out of this mess might be:

#1: *Don't hit.* her or me.

#2: Pray to want to love and understand her.

I'm really looking forward to the rush of peace and happiness that I know will come as I untangle this dilemma.

How do I know it will show up?

Because . . . I've been here many times before.

20

Dangerous Rules

Unbelievable as it sounds and horrifying as it is, we live much of our lives governed by rules and assumptions we created as toddlers. No wonder we experience chaos and confusion.

When little, we demanded that the world be a happy and satisfying place. To us that meant all of our needs and wants should and would be taken care of perfectly and immediately. It didn't take long to register that we'd landed in the wrong place if that was our expectation. So, in a panic, we settled for second best. If we couldn't have everything we wanted when we wanted it, then at least we wanted to be absolutely free of pain. To make sure that happened we devised strategies which then became rules. These rules sank deep inside, beyond our consciousness. They remain there into adulthood controlling our life's events until we uproot them.

How does this work? Something *bad* happens to us as a little one. It can be a big trauma or something that builds up over time. It doesn't matter if, from an objective standpoint, it is or isn't truly bad . . . from our perspective it's bad. Just based on the fact that our parents are human gives us a bundle of experiences to work from. Then, with our child's logic, we generalize that if it happened in this particular situation, it will happen in all situations with all people. Based on that conclusion, we devise a plan so that we won't ever be hurt by that circumstance again. Then, it all goes underground and we never connect our experiences with the outlandish rules we created when we could barely walk.

For example:

A child craves their parent's love and lets them know it. For whatever reason, the parents are unresponsive. It's a devastating blow. The conclusion of the child is, "If I open my heart to others I'll get hurt." The erroneous solution is, " I will stay closed off to avoid ever feeling that pain again." Sadly, that approach can chase love away for a lifetime.

A child lives in a controlling household. When they speak up they are teased, insulted or physically punished. The conclusion is, "If I speak up, I'll experience pain." The plan to avoid that pain is, "I'll never speak up again." It's then programmed into the control panel and produces all manner of negative results in their lives not only as children but also as adults.

Getting in touch with these conclusions and rules is liberating. So much finally makes sense after we uncover the beliefs that drive our life plan. As aware adults, we can finally be the one in the driver's seat of our lives instead of operating from the logic of a little kid who can't even reach the pedals.[8]

8 Pathwork Lecture 38 Images and Pathwork Lecture 41 The Damage They Do

21

Challenge the Rules

The only way to get free from the immature conclusions and dangerous rules that live below consciousness and continue to control your life is to become acquainted with them. You know you've got a few to tackle if you've tried to overcome some faults and found it impossible to change—no matter what you do. If there are recurring themes or fears you can't shake with logic consider trying this approach.

Make a list of the problems, conflicts and disappointments in your life. This is a job that takes patience and courage. It might take a while and it might change over time.

At first you may not see connections. Persevere and continue to look for common patterns. If you find yourself stuck, ask for help. Then keep your eyes and ears open. Help will show up in a surprising variety of ways. It might come from a random comment from a friend, an inspiration during meditation or prayer, something you see on a walk, or lyrics from a song. Be on the alert. It can come from any number of unexpected sources.

As a start, look for patterns in:

relationships
money issues
self worth
fear of failure
fear of success

When you've found an area of your life where you see patterns, try to identify what wrong conclusions you drew as a child. Follow those to the "solutions" you came up with in order to avoid feeling pain.

A way I've found that works for me is to, as honestly as possible, fill in the blanks of this statement no matter how outlandish it sounds.

"If I __________, I will ____________, so, I will __________ to avoid feeling pain."

Some examples:

"If I make a mistake, I'll be rejected by others, so, I'll be perfect to avoid feeling the pain of rejection."

"If I connect with someone it has to be all about them with no room for me, so, I'll never get close to anyone."

"If I have money others will take advantage of me, so, I'll make sure I don't have money to avoid feeling that pain."

The next step is to welcome the understanding of

your child's logic which led to these irrational beliefs with their accompanying "solutions." Often, as we realize the mistaken conclusions we drew that have guided much of our lives, we shove them aside. With an embarrassed laugh we sputter, "Oh c'mon. I can't possibly think that for heavens sake. It's not reasonable, it's not logical . . ." Of course it isn't. Remember, that reasoning was done by a toddler who had no other way to deal with the disillusionment and pain that life brings. It got buried underground in the unconscious because it had nowhere else to go.

When you're not aware of your irrational rules for life you don't have a choice about how you behave. You work automatically from these erroneous beliefs. By uncovering them, you create choice. You can stay stuck in your hurtful patterns or you can begin to discover the damage these faulty conclusions have brought into your life. The pattern is interrupted as soon as you realize it exists. Now you can choose to couple that awareness with actions that will guide you in a different direction.

One action you can take is to challenge your thinking by formulating a correct concept.

Write it down. Then compare it with your mistaken belief.

For example:

If the erroneous belief is:

"If I connect with someone it has to be all about them with no room for me."

A correct concept might be:

"If I connect with someone I might be able to strike a balance between my needs and their needs."

If the mistaken belief is:

"If I make a mistake, I'll be rejected by others."

A correct concept could be:

"If I make a mistake, others might think I'm just fine anyway."

If the erroneous belief is:

"If I have money others will take advantage of me."

A correct concept might be:

"It might be possible to welcome abundance and protect myself appropriately."

When you discover an erroneous belief ask yourself, "Is this true?" The answer to that question is guaranteed to lead you to a correct concept if you are willing to listen to the answer.[9]

9 Pathwork Lectures #39 Image Finding and #40: More on Image Finding A Summary

22

I Want to Want To

There are times when I'm acutely aware that I'm working against my own best interests. Yet, I find myself continuing to do whatever I'm doing over and over again. Beating myself up about it doesn't fix it. Pretending I don't care that I'm doing it doesn't change anything. Feeling guilty doesn't make any difference. Using all my reasoning powers doesn't work either.

There is however one action that is guaranteed to change things. I can choose to put my "I want to want to" prayer into play. Let's say I'm angry with someone and I can feel I really don't want to let go of it. My prayer in that instance is, "I want to want to give up feeling angry with them."

Sometimes I know I'm not even close to wanting to release whatever has this stranglehold on me. That's when I need to pull out the heavier ammunition of the "I want to want to want to..." prayer. Applied to my anger it would be "I *want* to *want* to *want* to heal my anger."

This is an effective way to reduce or, with persistence, even eliminate our resistance to change.

23

Getting Rid of Guilt

It's a hard thing for us to accept that we have a shadowy, lower part of ourselves that behaves badly.

We feel guilty about its misbehavior, so we try to deal with this aspect of ourselves in a variety of ways. One is to try to shove it out of sight and pretend it isn't there. Or, we attempt to make it go away through will power and self-control. Or, we can try to shame ourselves into behaving correctly.

But this darker side of us doesn't go away does it? And, if we behave better, it doesn't last, does it?

When we realize none of our strategies will work and we're stuck with this lower self, we try to make amends. There are as many ways of ineffectively trying to make up for this side of ourselves as there are people working to deal with it. We all have our custom-designed ways of trying to atone for this supposedly undesirable part of us.

The great news is there's an effective way to get out of this painful mess.

It's critical to understand that this lower self part of us

is actually divine energy that's been twisted through misconceptions and erroneous beliefs. This is why getting acquainted with what we think and believe is so important. It gives us the possibility of straightening out the kinks so that the energy can once again flow the way it was intended to flow.

Only when we're aware of our damaging ideas about life, do we have an opportunity to turn them around. When we use our willpower to make the choice to live fully, we live life with integrity. No more hiding. We're on our way to fulfillment and with that, no more guilt. There is nothing to atone for. We're doing our best. Yes, we'll stumble along the way. When we trip in the tangles, we'll understand and have compassion for ourselves. And, as long as we're doing our best, it is the most we can ever do. And, it is absolutely enough.[10]

10 Pathwork Lecture #108: Fundamental Guilt For Not Loving—Obligations

24

Connection

This morning I made plans with several friends . . . golf with a group this evening, a catch up dinner with another for tomorrow, a walk with yet another later this week. On top of that, last week I had dinner with friends, went to a concert with some other pals and joined another group for cards. Plus, just answering my e-mail took a chunk of time.

This may not be unusual for you. To me it's incredible because I lived with soul-searing loneliness for a very long time. I had arrived at a point where I didn't think I could survive the pain of it any longer.

How, I marvel today, did I transform from that sad, broken orphan into someone who has a life rich with connections?

The answer is that I connected with myself. I connected through giving myself the luxury of listening to what I was saying to me. I started paying close attention to what my brain and soul and history were whispering to me.

As I listened, my life began to change. I gained some

self-confidence. I didn't feel as frightened of life and people and events. I was willing to risk my heart a bit. I was willing to feel the thrill of being bright. I was willing to feel awkward if I didn't have something insightful or glamorous to say during a conversation. I was willing to take a peek at the witty side of me. I was willing to see the part of me that connects with another's heart.

I know now that my scorching loneliness was a result of disconnection from myself. Once I took my own hand, my life began to fill up not from the outside where I had been mistakenly looking, but from the inside. As always, my outer life eventually matched the fullness of my inner.[11]

11 Pathwork Lecture 77, "Self Confidence, its True Origin, and What Prohibits It."

25

Anxiety and Hopelessness

We unknowingly harbor two false beliefs that create a great deal of anxiety in us. One belief is that the world must bend to our will in order for us to be safe and happy. The other is that we will never have our desires met. These exist side by side. The result is that we experience uncertainty, anger, tension, anxiety, struggle and doubt.

To find your way to security, you need to become aware that this forcing current and this hopeless current exist in you simultaneously. Become acquainted with your voice that says, "I must have," on one hand and your voice that says, "I fear I won't get," on the other.

The part of you that *demands* your wishes be fulfilled is asking in a way that closes off the energy that would help manifest what it is you're requesting. The side of you that believes you won't get what you want is actually tuned into the truth. No, you won't get what you want when you ask this way. You need to find another approach.

The way to abolish hopelessness and anxiety is to release the fearful, demanding, tension-ridden voice that says to the Universe, "You *must* deliver what I think I have to have!!", and replace it with a gentler energy that says, "I'd like to have this if it's good for me. I'm willing to do what I need to do as my contribution to making this happen. Also help me realize it's not the end of the world if I don't get it. Help me cope if I need extra help. And help me really enjoy it if I do get what I'm asking for."

Only when you are aware that these two currents are at work in you can you give them up. When you make the effort to release them you will be operating from your true self . . . the one that provides solid self-confidence, true hope and safety.

26

Impatience

I woke up this morning feeling frightened and angry. I had the gnawing flutter of panic that comes when I feel I have nowhere to be safe. As a nation, actually as a world, we are staring into the face of wars, recession, deep economic instability and a seeming lack of effective world leadership.

As I awoke with that familiar flutter of panic trying to take hold of me, somewhere deep inside I felt a different flutter next to the panic. It was the tender thought that I have a choice. Perhaps I don't have to be in tears and anxiety and unknowing. Maybe there's another route to take that leads me toward peace.

As I settled in to contact my deeper knowing, an angry, impatient voice from the street interrupted shouting, "Hurry up! Hurry up!" It happened to be an older brother trying to get his little sister to school on time. I realized I sometimes approach my panicky states in a similar way by shouting or whispering, "Hurry up! Hurry up!"

I used to think the reason I couldn't connect with my inner wisdom at those times was because my soul retreated from me when I was impatient. Today I see a different picture. My soul is there sturdy and strong quite ready to help me out of the swamp. However, my insistent, fear-driven urging of "Hurry up!!," has tossed a hand grenade into the mix creating debris, rubble and confusion which makes it hard to hear the wisdom that's available.

I'm realizing today that what I need to do is honor my fear, anger and impatience. Be with it. Feel it. Be with me in compassion. Take my own hand and listen to me. Listen to that small one inside me who is so frightened of today and tomorrow. Once she can share her fears instead of trying to blast them away with force, both of us will be able to hear the wisdom my soul would like to share.

27

Blame

What is blame?

Blame: assign fault, place responsibility for something *wrong* on another

Blaming Ourselves

We pay lip service to the fact that mistakes are a normal part of life, but often, deep inside, we have the whip in hand.

One reason we blame ourselves is that we find it just plain unacceptable to be human. We believe that to be okay in life, we need to be perfect. When we don't meet our self-imposed standards of perfection, we berate ourselves.

Sometimes the darker side of us likes the high drama of breast-beating, wailing, self-blame. And, along with the fun of the drama, if we're busy blaming ourselves for something, we're not really taking responsibility—we're just pretending to.

It takes a great deal of humility and courage to look at

ourselves as we really are in all our magnificence and imperfections. It takes a lot of love to accept our very human selves.

Blaming Others

Blaming others is high on everyone's list of temptations.

Why do we do blame others?

> We want to feel superior to them.
>
> We hope it gets us off the hook from having to do anything about the situation.
>
> We hope it keeps us from getting into trouble
>
> We mistakenly believe that if we can hold someone else accountable for something gone wrong, then we can hold them responsible for making it go right.
>
> Our pride says, "I can't be wrong; it has to be you."
>
> Our fear says, "You have to make me safe and I'm not feeling that way right now."
>
> Our will says, "It must be the way I want. It isn't right now, so I demand you fix it."

Blame separates us from others. It attempts to place responsibility for our well being into someone else's hands where it doesn't belong. Doing the work of finding where we blame others for our unhappiness helps dissolve our pain. In addition, it helps us hold others with compassion and love when they lash out in blame at us. It heals us both.

28

The Road to Freedom

Facing our fears brings security and safety.

Feeling our loneliness creates the capacity to have fulfillment, love and

companionship

Finding our hopelessness makes space for true and justified hope.

Knowing our hatred allows us to truly love.

Discovering our weaknesses builds up our strengths.

Experiencing our pain opens the path towards peace.[12]

---

12 Pathwork Lecture #190: Importance of Feeling All Feelings Including Fear

29

"Forgot Your Dry Cleaning Again?"

I have a favorite reminder that help is always there for not only the big-ticket items but the little things too and comes even when I forget to ask for it

I had one of those go-to outfits that saw more than its fair share of action during the jam-packed summer I transitioned from working for a large company to my own independent speaking and consulting practice. It was the uniform to grab without even thinking. I had worn this favorite to a Friday speech where some mysterious stain had jumped on my lapel. So, I dropped it off at the dry cleaner's on my way home from the convention center, planning to pick it up after work on Monday in order to be able to wear it to a 7 AM meeting on Tuesday.

As I pulled into my driveway Monday night, looking forward to a quick bite to eat before I headed out to my evening event, I noticed something on my front door. Attached to a hanger was an advertisement asking, "Forgot your dry cleaning again?" Well, yes indeed I had. Not even needing to get out of the car since the print was big enough for me to see from my car,

I zipped off to the dry cleaners, enjoyed a nice snack and had my lucky jacket for the Tuesday morning wake-up meeting.

I framed the ad and ever since that day it sits where I see it first thing in the morning. It's a terrific reminder that help is there for all sizes of challenges not just the big things and not only when I remember to ask.

30

Duality

Have you ever caught yourself in a tussle that feels like you're fighting to the death over something that in the overall scheme of things is fairly insignificant? And even if you are tuned in to the outlandishness of the situation, do you still feel the compulsion to battle until you can declare victory?

That's one crazy effect of living in the prison of duality.

Duality is experiencing life in terms of all *or* nothing. It means all you *or* all me, total happiness *or* total unhappiness, totally right *or* totally wrong, all good *or* all bad. There is a constant undercurrent of fear and straining away from the undesirable coupled with the straining toward the desirable. This is an experience filled with perpetual pain and anxiety.

Why are we trapped in this horrible place?

As infants, we remember with our soul memory that it's possible to have all of our needs met all of the time and feel totally happy. We mistakenly believe that we can reproduce that state here on earth. As we experience life as it is, we find that sometimes our needs are met and sometimes they're not. Sometimes we're happy and sometimes unhappy. Because the memory of what it's like to be happy all of the time is still so strong for us, we try everything in our power to make that happen again. We also apply this idea to the other side of the coin. We believe that if we are not in total pleasure we will be in total "unpleasure." In our young consciousness we equate total "unpleasure" with pain and oblivion and that belief fuels a struggle that will torture us until we break the chain.

This is a tough one to even consider because our egos are saying, "How ridiculous. I'm a reasonable person. I don't have to have everything go my way *all* of the time." But, observe your emotions. When you feel that desire to stomp someone into the ground who tries to tell you that you're wrong—that's what duality feels like. When you feel anxiety mounting in a situation to the point where you think you'll jump out of your skin—that's duality at work. When you get so depressed you can hardly get off the couch that's duality driving the bus.

Do we have to stay in this prison? Of course we don't.. How do we get out? First, set the intention to be in touch with that reactive part of you. Then, observe yourself and your reactions. How often do you find yourself acting as if it is a matter of you *or* me, right *or* wrong, good *or* bad?

Experiment with correct and incorrect concepts. Instead

of telling yourself it's you *or* me, try saying, "It's you *and* me." Instead of clinging to "I'm right/you're wrong" in a conflict, try searching for where you're both right *and* you're both wrong. Instead of demanding, "It *must* be this way." Try telling yourself, "It *could* be this way *and* it *could* be another way."

The result through intention, time and focus will be that you accept that you live in a "sometimes" world. This acceptance means you'll be at peace knowing that you'll have your needs met some of the time and some of the time you won't. You'll be more than fine knowing you'll be happy as well as unhappy. You won't be torturing yourself by straining toward the impossible goal of total satisfaction and happiness all the time and away from the fear that if you don't get it all you will be destroyed.

Finally, you will be able to hold it all in its enormity with strength and self-confidence[13]

---

13 From Pathwork Lectures: #81: Conflicts in the World of Duality #143: Unity and Duality

31

Broken Heart

I have good news. I'm living peacefully with a broken heart this morning. In my younger, less wise days I did anything to scramble back from feeling this kind of pain.

It's good to know that I won't die from this although the crushed feeling is very heavy. It's good to know that there is something I can learn from this. It's sweet to have a friend call to check in with me for support. It's good to know that I can live in this world with its joy and heartache, pain and pleasure, goodness and badness and not fight, fight, fight to experience only joy, only pleasure only goodness and only happiness.

Life is all of the above and now that I've learned to embrace that fact, I feel so much safer.

32

Tending

A few weeks ago I got rid of huge bundles of grapevines from my backyard. After conferring with my gardening friends, I made a plan for what I'd plant in that newly cleared space that I thought would be wonderful and beautiful. Then . . . life got awfully busy.

One day, as I took a moment to look up from this busy life, I saw that unplanned growth had taken root in the space I had cleaned up not that long ago. It was almost as crowded as it had been in the pre-grapevine removal days.

Here is nature once again teaching me an important lesson about my spiritual life.

I had cleared out some aggressive and destructive growth. I had intended to use that area to create beauty and pleasure and then I neglected to do the work to make that happen. It's the same when we do our work of uprooting misconceptions and distorted beliefs. We create space for something. If we don't take advantage of that opportunity to consciously create what we'd like to have in our lives it can be like my backyard . . . filled with damaging growth that sneaks up on us before we know it.

We need to tend our inner lives like I needed to tend my newly available patch of backyard. Instead of just breathing a big sigh of relief after finishing that piece of tough work, figuring it would stay clear until I could get to it with my great plan, I needed to tend it a lot more diligently.

If I had paid attention and noticed what had started to grow in this space, I could have removed it a bit at a time and not allowed anything to root very deeply. Instead, it looks like I have a bundle of work ahead of me . . . again.

A bit of time each day paying attention to what is trying to take root will keep you uncluttered until you deliberately plant what you actually want to create.

33

Making a Change

We have amazing insights. We come up with great ideas about how we want our lives to be different based on those incredible insights. And then . . . nothing changes. Sigh, , , , we say, "See, this stuff doesn't work."

Actually it does work and very nicely. We just need to give making a change a bit of practical help.

A trick of our lower selves when we uncover an erroneous belief or a misconception that's been causing trouble for us, is to whisper, "Whew! Good work. Nice job. Really good effort. Now, let's hurry up and get moving on to the next challenge." Our darker side wants to hustle us quickly on to the next piece of work because without cementing new behaviors to support that fresh insight, its positive impact could float away like dandelion fluff in a spring breeze.

After doing the work of uncovering a belief that leads us into trouble and pain, there is a four-part formula that guarantees change:

Set your intention.

Pray for help.

Choose and use a reminder of your desire to change that can be readily visible to you at all times.

Use it.

For example:

After considerable work, a friend had uncovered how mean and nasty she could be toward herself. She set an intention to be kinder whenever she could. She said her prayers for help. Then, to serve as a reminder of her desire to change, she treated herself to a beautiful ring which she didn't take off until being kinder to herself became more her usual pattern.

By setting intention, praying for help and adding a practical reminder that you want to bring something wonderful into your life, the changes you want are guaranteed to come about.

34

I'd Rather Not Today

This morning there are things going on in my life I'd rather not face. I don't want to know that a rift with someone has anything to do with me. I don't want to face my fears and greed and lack of faith as I struggle to make some hard financial decisions. Even though I know when I face the truth there is tremendous relief . . . this morning I still don't want to go there.

The best I can do today is pray, "Help me be willing to look at the truth." And, . . .that's enough.

35

A Time for Each

To create the life we want, we need to realize that there is an appropriate time for action and there's an appropriate time for waiting.

We can chase away things we want by taking action when it's the time to be still and patient. We muddy up the works just as much by sitting back when it's actually time for us to be on the move.

Being in tune with ourselves gives us guidance about when we should be forging ahead and when we should be patiently waiting.[14]

14 Pathwork Lecture: #55: Three Cosmic Principles: The Expanding, Restricting and Static

36

The Big Three

We all have a trio within designed to rob us of happiness. Self-will, false pride and fear tangle together to trip us up over and over again.

Self will is the tyrant that demands what she wants when she wants it and will do anything to make that happen.

False pride is a minefield that has nothing to do with real pride. Real pride is the feeling of dignity that comes from truly knowing your worth. False pride is a bogus feeling of worth that comes only when we can convince ourselves that we're better than others, smarter than others, more successful than others, more attractive than others. It's a house of cards that keeps collapsing.

Fear is the feeling of impending danger that's activated when you feel that the demands of your self-will and pride won't be met.

Standing on their own, each of these is painful enough. When they feed on each other, they generate a debilitating energy that sabotages your best intentions.

You can release yourself from this pain-filled place by first accepting without judgment or criticism that these exist in you as part of the temporary reality created by your darker side. With this acceptance, light immediately penetrates and begins to weaken them.

Another step to strip this trio of their power is to separate them from one another. Standing on their own, they lack the ferocity that is generated by the interaction. Begin by working to untangle them. Focus on becoming aware of your false pride, your demanding self will and your fear as separate energy currents.

A great place to start is to face the voice that wants you to think all this applies to others but certainly not you. That's false pride at work. To weaken it, ask your Higher Self to help you summon the courage to be willing to consider another possibility. Ask to know the truth about whether this could possibly apply to you *just like everyone else*.

Then, feel the clenched-fistedness of "I want what I want when I want it." Just feel it without judgment. Accepting that part of you—that young unresolved part of you that is so unreasonably demanding—begins immediately to dissolve its poison.

Your feelings of fear will lessen as your demands driven by the will-filled tyrant and your false pride lessen. As a result of this work, the big three will have much less of a stranglehold on you and you will eventually be freed from their grip.[15]

15 From Pathwork Lecture:#30: Self Will, Pride and Fear

37

I Want What I Want When I Want It

It was quite a relief to discover the tiny red headed tyrant that lives within me. She wants what she wants when she wants it and figures no one should stand in her way. When people do seem to stand in her way, she doubles down her efforts to make sure she gets what she wants NOW!! We all have one of these tender little tots inside us who stomps those tiny feet and pouts and cries with abandon in an effort to bend the world to their will.

I was actually delighted to meet her. Why?

First of all, accepting that she exists takes away the strain of trying to hide her from me and everyone else.

Second, I don't have to be afraid of her acting out anymore because accepting that she lives in me puts me in the driver's seat. When I was working hard to not acknowledge that she lived in me, I would unconsciously draw on a variety of manipulative tricks to get my way. For example, I'd try to get others to feel sorry for me or try to make them feel guilty so they'd give me what I wanted. Sometimes I'd give them what they wanted, not because I wanted to, but in order to have them owe me something. All the while guilt and anxiety were building within me.

Now, when I feel that demanding energy bubble up, I don't try to tamp her down or shove her away or try to get my desires met in a sneaky way. I treat this strong emotion with the respect and attention it deserves.

To release the tension of the moment, I often let her blow. This doesn't mean that I irresponsibly unload my feelings. I have a couple of different approaches depending on the circumstances. When I need to keep the explosion under wraps, I let her have her foot stomping tantrum in my mind. Other times I have the luxury of privacy. Then I'll grab a tennis racquet and whale the living daylights out of an ancient couch in my basement. That's when I let words fly out of my mouth uncensored too. It's amazing what I learn about what I'm really thinking when I do that. It often helps me discover the root of what's going on to cause such strong emotion.

After I had gotten used to her popping up at even the most awkward times, a great thing happened. The simple recognition from me that I was having an *I-want-what-I want- when-I-want-it moment* took the pressure off immediately. I could finally greet that feisty Little One with acceptance instead of fear and judgment and I could get to the heart of the matter much more quickly. My reactions in the moment didn't serve to make the situation worse as they often had in the past.

In fact now things are frequently resolved very nicely right on the spot.

38

Meeting Evil

It's critical to consider how evil works because we can't deal with an enemy whose existence we ignore and whose weapons we don't recognize. The more we know about evil the less of an influence it will have in our lives.

Evil doesn't glide up in a flashy stretch limo and announce its arrival. It rolls into town under the radar in a family sedan with a couple of dents in it. The danger lies in it looking so ordinary.

One way evil works its dark charms is to convince us that we are separate and isolated. Evil whispers that it is a choice between you *or* me. It convinces us that another's pain is not our pain. It numbs us. Cruelty toward others and ourselves is one result of this numbness. Evil works to keep us separate from our real source of power and peace . . . that true home that lies within us.

Another way evil insinuates itself into our lives is by convincing us that all we can trust is what we can hear, see, taste, smell or touch. It works hard to make us believe that nothing exists beyond this material world, which leads us to live in a disconnected way.

A third way evil manifests is through half truths, confusion and distortion. We are driven crazy trying to sort it out. Because it's so difficult and such a strain, we give up and give in instead of asking the question that really cuts through all the garbage which is, "What is the truth here?"

The way to conquer evil is to face it squarely. Know there is more than what we see and experience on the surface. Work diligently toward connection. Never give up asking the question "What is the truth?" This is the way to our true selves that hold all the peace, security and happiness we could ever imagine and more. It's no accident that evil is the word, *live* spelled backwards.

39

Worry

I find myself worrying a lot lately about people I love.

It's dawning on me that worrying is actually adding anxiety, fear and lack of faith into the situation instead of helping in any way. I think the best thing I can do in my haze of pain is to bless.

What do I mean by bless? Giving a blessing is inviting the best in. It's praying for grace for everyone involved. Blessing is praying for what I think would be a good solution and then praying to surrender to what is right whether it's what I want or not. Giving a blessing is asking for divine care and protection.

Bless. Bless. Bless.

In my helplessness . . . bless.

In my love . . . bless.

In my fear . . . bless.

In my impatience for all of us to be out of pain . . . bless.

In faith . . . bless.

In doubt . . . bless.

10

It's Mostly about Me

It turns out that when we're upset with someone, it isn't their fault that we feel angry, hurt, embarrassed or any other unsettling emotion. Their actions, even negative ones, wouldn't have an impact on us if what they said or did didn't strike a chord of recognition within.

For example, on a weekend getaway, one of my pals let me know that, in her opinion, I took too much time in the bathroom. I felt hurt and angry and wanted to lash out. I was tempted to make it about her by finding *good* reasons why she was wrong and I was right as well as an abundance of examples of where she was more inconsiderate than I was etc., etc., etc. . . .. Instead, I took a deep breath and created a quiet moment to see if I could figure out why I had such an extreme reaction to something that was fairly insignificant.

I chose to do this because I wanted to feel better and the best way I've learned to deal with these experiences is to ask to know what I can learn from what happened. It's not a mistake when we get triggered. There's a reason our spirit drew that experience to us. Do your soul the nurturing favor of honestly asking, "Why did I attract this incident?" "What not only can I learn, but even more importantly, what do I *need* to learn from this?" "What is asking to be healed?"

In this case, my first realization was that I felt guilty and anxious about inconveniencing someone. Asking, "Why?" led me to unearth my buried fear that there's no room for what I want and need. That paved the way to my up-until-then unconscious belief that the "right and safe" way to be in life was to be solely concerned about another person's desires . . . never mine. Then I let it sink in how enraged and hurt my young one felt about this "rule." That's the part of me that wanted to lash out and hurt my friend.

Once I identified why I had such an intense reaction, I was free to look at the truth of the matter. I no longer needed to be trapped functioning from the wounded Little One who felt such pain at not being given her rightful space. I could respond to life from present day reality not from hidden beliefs that lingered from my history.

So instead of adding tension to the house party by striking out from the part of me that felt frightened and hurt, I learned something important about myself that served me well for a lot longer than that weekend. Searching for where it's about us, not them, gives us a lot of control in situations that hurt and a way to get free of pain.

Sometimes I have such a strong reaction that I need to spend time first asking for the humility and courage to ask those questions. The marvelous beauty of this soul growth is that it's foolproof. The answer will come with the attendant peace and freedom that always accompanies learning the truth.

41

A Matter of Perspective

The lens through which we filter our lives is powerful.

In a conversation with a friend long ago (pre GPS times) I made the comment that I felt frustrated and inadequate because I'd always get lost when trying to locate someplace new.

She commented with a great deal of self-confidence, even bragging a bit, "I never get lost. I can always zero in within a mile of where I'm supposed to be."

Interestingly, the reason I said I always got lost was that I could easily get within a mile of where I wanted to be but not to the exact location on my first try.

Same experience—we both got within a mile of our destinations on the first try.

Two different perspectives about what that meant—one producing a powerful outlook, the other, a crippling one.

42

Holding It All

Some big changes are going on in my life right now that I don't particularly like. I initiated none and all are impacting me a lot. A lot of exciting things that I like are going on in my life at the same time. Result? I'm a swirl of emotions bumping up against each other. One minute I have tears leaking out, a few hours later my heart is dancing.

I'm so grateful that one of the results of stepping on to a path of self-awareness is building the ability to hold it all . . . no matter how big, no matter how intense, no matter how mutually exclusive the emotions appear to be. I'm grateful for this capacity because I no longer stress myself by trying to run away from my mixture of sadness, excitement, fear, hope, disappointment, delight, anger, grief and pleasure.

I used to run from the sadness, anger, and grief because it hurt. I turned from hope and excitement because I didn't want to feel disappointment. I ran from fear because I didn't want to feel helpless. I avoided feeling happy because it didn't seem right to feel that way when I was so sad about other things. I used to run away from feeling any of these things because it was so overwhelming sometimes. One result of this running was a build-up of toxins that damaged me and leaked out in poisonous ways to wound others and pollute our circumstances.

Now I can hold it all a lot of the time. This is a hard-won skill that I'm delighted and proud to have earned. Instead of adding difficulty to situations by trying to escape through tamping down my feelings, now there is a flow which cleanses and soothes and brings the best I can offer to tough times.

43

You Can't Go Home Again . . . Although You Try and Try and Try

We unconsciously re-create our childhood hurts over and over with one great and desperate goal in mind. We want things to turn out differently than they did in the past. In our attempt to accomplish this, we basically turn everyone into a version of Mom and Dad. If Mom and Dad didn't value us, we unconsciously seek out people who don't value us now so that we can convince them that we do in fact have worth. If we had a childhood of loneliness, we may lead a hectic, overscheduled life now to convince others and ourselves that we are likable and popular. If we feel we were treated as stupid, we're driven to convince the rest of the world and ourselves that we're not.

Unfortunately this strategy doesn't deliver soothing medicine. Instead, this re-creation creates nasty and pain-filled fallout.

In this attempt to create a different ending for our story, our loneliness grows and intensifies. This happens because we aren't seeing others as who they are. We project qualities and faults and powers on them that aren't necessarily theirs.

Fear, depression, and anxiety escalate because it feels that our lives are out of control.

No matter what we do, no matter how hard we try, life isn't turning out the way we want it to. Confusion and pain grow.

The way out of this purgatory is to get acquainted with who you are. Work to connect how what you do now relates to what was lacking or caused hurt for you when you were younger.

Find out what you want. Find out how you stand in your own way that prevents you from having what you want. Learn to make the connection between what your beliefs are and what's happening in your life.

Having the courage to do this gives you control of your life. You will create from a conscious place. Finally you can live a life you love.[16]

16 Pathwork Lecture: #73: Compulsion To Recreate and Overcome Childhood Hurts

11

Forgot to Be Grateful

This morning I'm really angry. I'm foot-stomping, dish-throwing, door-kicking angry. I woke up that way and I'm building up a head of steam. I'm storming as I toss in a load of laundry. I hate the snow, I hate my Visa bill, I am fuming about the crowded schedule I have today.

Thank goodness help has arrived. It's exhausting to be that ticked off.

Pouring a cup of coffee, I hear the rumble of the small snowplow which belongs to the company that's taken care of my snow removal needs for years. The truck's arrival triggers the thought that I'm so miserable lately because I'm forgetting to be grateful.

As I think more about it, I realize I've been so busy concentrating on what's wrong and what I perceive I don't have that I'm letting much of my bounty go unnoticed and unappreciated. I'm moaning and groaning about yet another snowstorm that hit us with six more inches of the white stuff—feels unrelenting this year. We are in the midst of a recession and wars, I'm pressed for time today, I'm just plain worried about my future and I'm not sleeping very well.

Why am I so focused on the negative lately? I think it's because I want to be rescued, plain and simple. I'm scared and I want someone to make it all better. So I hope, using the child's logic buried within my little scared self, that if I build things up to make them seem really, really bad, maybe someone will notice and do something about it. My anger is my adult temper tantrum trying to force the Universe to deliver the happiness I demand RIGHT NOW and, by doing that, make this scared, awful feeling in my stomach go away.

Well, the rescue has come after all hasn't it? Not in the form of another person splashing money all over me or making the snow go away for the rest of the winter but in the form of remembering I have much to be grateful for even in the things I'm complaining about.

I do have someone to make the snow go away—at least in my little section of the world. I had budgeted money for the holiday expenses that are now showing up on my credit card so that's not such a big deal after all. I'm tight on time because my day is filled with activities I'm looking forward to including preparing for a visit from my grandsons tomorrow. It's actually pretty nice to be in a time bind for these reasons. When I feel gratitude, I feel my whole self—body and soul—totally relax. It's nice to realize that I have a choice where I focus my attention. It's great to know that one of the choices I can make will get me out of my misery.

45

Nice Surprise!!

Someone tried to pin some blame on me the other day. Things weren't going the way my companion wanted them to and I was handy so I got the hit.

At the time I felt really good about how I responded to the blame. Later, I realized I was pleasantly surprised about it too.

In the past, I would have gotten defensive and flustered and ticked off that I was being blamed for something that I didn't feel was my fault. I might have tried to point out how I didn't really have anything to do with the situation at hand and that actually it was more about her influence than me and on and on and on.

This time, I didn't feel any of those jolts of defensive energy. Instead I found myself thinking without blaming, "Wow, you really have a need to blame." Then I heard me offer to remove myself from the situation. I didn't think I was contributing much to the problem at hand but I was willing to get out of the way just in case I was. All this was done without resentment, ill will or anger.

How did this turn-around happen and why was it a surprise to me?

The turn-around from defensiveness and counter-attack happened because I try to make it a habit to investigate what's going on for me when I have a reaction to a person or situation that feels not quite right or is just plain painful. Among my many discoveries was the realization that I had a tendency to blame. That led me to try to understand why I wanted to do that. Learning more about why I chose to blame helped me understand others so much better too. As I eventually found compassion for myself in the place where I want to blame, it led me to have compassion for others when they blame me.

It felt like a surprise that day because the healing response is often gentle and incremental. I'd been gradually and surely moving into a space of understanding and compassion around blame for quite a while. That day, everything came together to help me see the results of my work in one fell swoop. I love it when that happens.

16

The Answer Will Come

A friend and I were chatting about how irritating it is to the darker forces when we have confidence that the answer will come. When we know that eventually the solution to our dilemma or question will arrive, we wait with a patience and receptivity that actually speeds up the arrival of the response. This is a truth our dark side would definitely prefer us to not know.

17

Setting Intention

Setting intention is like setting the sails on a boat. It aims us in the direction we want to go and captures the wind that will give us the power to get there.

Setting intention is clearly and concisely stating your goal.

Some examples are:

> My intention is to give my best.
>
> My intention is to connect with myself.
>
> My intention is to be kind to me.
>
> My intention is to love the person I can't stand right now.
>
> My intention is to learn about my negativity.
>
> My intention is to know that there is enough for everyone.
>
> My intention is to learn the truth.
>
> My intention is to accept and enjoy others.

By declaring your intention you call into play enormous resources and power to get you there.

48

Who Am I?

I am the tiny redheaded tyrant who wants what she wants when she wants it.

I am the loving friend who partners with another to face a bout with cancer.

I am the one who is courageous enough to risk my heart in relationship.

I am the one who yearns to feel safe in this world.

I am the one who is afraid there is not enough.

I am the one who knows beyond a shadow of a doubt there is more than enough for all.

I am the one who awkwardly stumbles through life.

I am the one who surrenders with grace.

I am the supremely confident one when I tap into my inner wisdom.

I am the frightened Little One hugging herself.

I am the one who hates my neighbor.

I am the one who loves my neighbor.

I am the one who is judgmental

I am the one who is accepting.

I am the one who knows we are one.

I am all these contradictory things at once.

I am mostly at peace with that.

About the Author

Tess Kirby is a Pathwork Helper, organizational consultant and leadership coach. She lives in Ann Arbor, Michigan. You can learn more about Tess at www.tesskirbypathwork.com and www.tesskirby.com.

CPSIA information can be obtained at www.ICGtesting.com
Printed in the USA
BVOW07s0839101214

378026BV00002B/2/P

9 781931 589710